Every
Word
You
Cannot
Say*

Every Word You Cannot Say*

IAIN S. THOMAS

Andrews McMeel
PUBLISHING®

Andrews McMeel Publishing
a division of Andrews McMeel Universal
1130 Walnut Street, Kansas City, Missouri 64106

www.andrewsmcmeel.com

www.iainsthomas.com
www.twitter.com/iwrotethisforu
www.instagram.com/iwrotethisforyou.me/

19 20 21 22 23 TEN 10 9 8 7 6 5 4 3 2 1

ISBN: 978-1-4494-9520-6

Library of Congress Control Number: 2018949443

Editor: Allison Adler
Production Editor: Amy Strassner
Production Manager: Tamara Haus

ATTENTION: SCHOOLS AND BUSINESSES
Andrews McMeel books are available at quantity discounts with bulk purchase
for educational, business, or sales promotional use. For information, please
e-mail the Andrews McMeel Publishing Special Sales Department:
specialsales@amuniversal.com.

Every Word You Cannot Say*

I don't know why, but I do not feel
like I'm like you, or anyone else.

I feel like I'm the only one who feels
the things I feel, or thinks the way I think.

I'm worried that I'm taking everything too
seriously, or not seriously enough.

Sometimes I want you to see me, and
sometimes I want to disappear.

I don't know if I've ever truly felt like
the ground beneath me was firm.

Things always feel like they're moving and
I never get the chance to catch up to them
and when I do, it feels like it all goes too quickly.

I am nice to people I don't like because
I don't know what else to do.

I feel like I'm waiting for something
but I don't know what it is.

I often walk past people in the street,
and I wonder if anyone else is waiting too.

I don't know if I'm ever, really, "Here."

So I'm fine.*

*I am not fine.

I don't know your name.

But I do know that it was beautiful to your mother and that the first time she said it, and decided it was yours, she smiled. I know she said it several times after that, like the words to a beautiful song only she knew. She tried it on like a beautiful summer day.

I do not know what you do for money, but I do know that sometimes, whatever it is, it's difficult. I do not know whether you are rich or poor, but I do know that regardless of how much money you have in the bank or how big your house is, numbers have never stopped the world from intruding on happiness.

And sometimes, things are hard.

I know that, once, someone touched your hand and
you did not want them to pull their hand away, but
they did and this made you sad. And for this reason, I
also know that sometimes you smile even when there's
nothing to smile about.

I know that the grass grew while you were sleeping.
I know that somewhere on the other side of the world,
the sun shone on people you will never meet.

I know that at least once, if not several times, someone
you knew woke up in the middle of the night thinking of
you and wondering what became of you.

And they've contemplated calling you
out of the blue.

I know you have a tiny scar on your body
that only you know about, that only you see now.

I know you remember how you got it.

I know your body will be cold, after you die
and that right now, while you're reading this,
is the only time I can guarantee it will be warm.

I know that the sun will rise every single day
until it doesn't, until there's no more reason to.

I know that time itself holds you tight.

I know that you get ink on your fingers and
don't know when it'll come off.

I know strangers can stain your heart
in the same way.

I know sometimes your brain is too loud
and your heart bangs on the ceiling with a
broom,
screaming,

"Shut up, you're going to ruin this for us."

I know sometimes, it's too late, and
the music plays on.

I know you hurt and that you love and that, sometimes, love is the reason you hurt.

I know you feel things and wish sometimes that someone was there to tell you that you're allowed to feel everything you're feeling.

I know that, sometimes, you wish someone would just say the words you needed to hear because, sometimes, you don't even know what those words are.

I feel what you're feeling, if you feel these things.

And I want you to know that despite how wrong everything seems right now, you are someone special, in someone else's story.

You are not reading this alone.

You are a part of so much.

Here:

When you're lost, take a brief
moment to find yourself.

In every moment.
In every breath.
In every star.
In every blade of grass.
In every lost toy.
In every forgotten song.
In every burnt map.
In every broken glass.
In every memory of perfume.
In every taste.
In every line.
In your heart.
In trust.

When you touch this page, someone else, somewhere else, is waiting to touch the exact same spot, and is thinking of you.

I promise you, someone, somewhere in the world is thinking of how beautiful you are on the inside, how much they wish that whatever is hurting you would stop, how much they love you without ever having known your name.

Reach out, and touch their heart.

Because somewhere, they are reaching out to yours.

Here.

I
want
to love
and be loved.
I want my chil-
dren to have a better life
than I did. I want my
dad to be proud of me
and I want him to say it. I
want to drink cold water
on a hot day. Some- times I
cry at some- thing that I
don't believe anyone else
cries at. There's a way that
clouds can move across the sky that
can do this to me. Sometimes I worry
about stupid things in the middle of the
night. I find it hard to talk to certain people
and I don't think I will ever really under- stand
why. My stomach hurts every now and again
and I'm convinced it's cancer or some- thing else
that's about to kill me. I still think about something
stupid I said in high school to impress someone. I still
think about every relationship I fucked up. I worry
about my mom, a lot. Sometimes I feel like I'm the
only one who cares about a lot of stuff. I'm just
trying to do the right thing, and I don't know
what that is. I think you have to make it
up new every single day.

Here.

Listen:

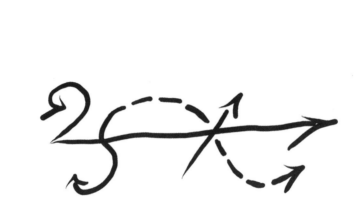

You are part of a beautiful story.

But "Chapter One" is not your first memory.

The first word in this story was written a long, long time ago.

And you are only in the story for just a few short pages.

But in these pages, you get to decide how the
story goes.

Over time, you will play every character in the story.

You will love and be loved.

You will hate and be hated.

You will be cruel and you will be kind.

You will start young and if you are lucky, you will be old when it ends.

Everyone you meet along the way is just someone at a different point in their story.

So be patient and kind.

But don't let anyone tell you how your story should go.

Only you know how your story goes.

And when your pages are over, don't be sad or angry.

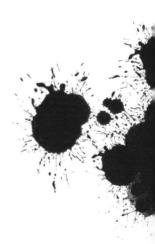

The wind does not stop being the wind
when   it   stops   blowing.

A wave does not stop being a wave when it

crashes

against the shore.

A story does not stop being a story when you turn
the page.

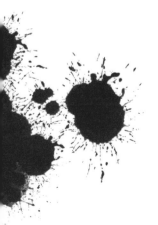

What have you lost between this page

and this one?

Every single life you touch, moves the story forward.

And so, if you're kind, your story becomes part of many stories.

But life is not special because of what happens after it's over.

Life is special because life is special.

Your story is special.

And whether you know it or not, you are adding new words to it every single day.

If things are good, they will change. If things are bad, they will change.

Because change is the nature of every story.

What words will you add to it today?

Let me tell you how the world becomes
better.

The world becomes better when good people like you look at themselves and decide what kind of life they want to live, and what they're willing to do to make it that way.

This does not mean you need to fight more.

It means you need to find ways to fight less.

Sometimes, our immediate response to the way the world is, is anger, and the world is the way it is, because sometimes our immediate response to it, is anger.

Wait for yourself,

and be patient with yourself and others.

Wait.

There's a kind of kindness that
can settle on your heart.

And Here?

Here:

You cannot say why you cannot forget the feeling
of their skin
against yours.

Here.

Here.

Here.

And point to the center of yourself.

And tap your sternum.

And touch your forehead.

And touch your tongue.

You cannot say that you are sorry they left, or that you
left them.

You cannot walk up to strangers in the street and say,
"Here is where it hurts."

And point to the center of yourself.

And tap your sternum.

And touch your forehead.

And touch your tongue.

You cannot tell them, "This is what it feels like,
like a pebble in a shoe you're not wearing."

You cannot say it is the absence of them, and the
presence of them, and the difference between those
two things, that hurts the most.

Here.

Here.

Here.

*

Here.

*

But when do we tell the truth
and say what must be said?

Only when the world ends?

We all think this a game we can win, and there will be
a moment when the game is over, when we can look at
each other and see each other's cards, and say everything
we meant to say when we were alive and we could speak.

"I fell in love with you and I never said anything."

"I hated you but I stayed."

"I just wanted you to know that what you did, hurt."

"Why couldn't you love me like I loved you?"

"Why did you leave?"

But there is no chance after this one.

(And I know you're worried about what it takes
to live, to speak, to start to feel better.)

It takes time.

But time is all it takes.

Not your heart. Not your life.

Just time.

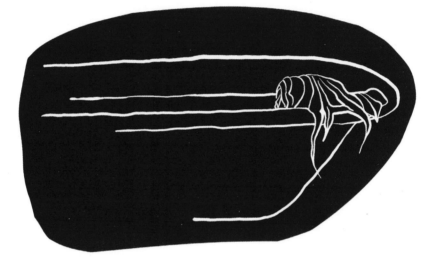

This is what no one tells you
about hurting people.

Sometimes we do not see how much someone is
already hurting

and so when we hurt

someone

just a little,

and they react,

we think they're overreacting, that they're hostile

and they think they're finally being brave.

You are not a moment.

Moments are just moments.

You are so much more.*

*We forget that how a person acts in each moment is not who they are, that each person is a series of moments and we cannot judge any moment in isolation, and use that moment to define them. It is not up to others, it is up to us, which moments we want to hang on to, for good or for bad. We forget our successes and enshrine our failures. We forget there is still a child in all of us, begging for love. We forget that this is true of every person we meet.

We only hear the loudest voices when really, we should be listening to the quietest.

But where is the goodness of the world?

There is room in the universe for much love, for those
who would put it there, for those with the patience and
goodness of heart to love, there is great peace in every
moment, if we only wait for it to leave our hearts,

like

an

overflowing

river.*

Here
Here
*Here

Here
  Here
    Here
      Here
      Here Here
        Here Here
          Here Here
            Here Here
              Here Here Here
                Here Here Here
                  Here Here Here
                    Here Here Here
                      Here Here Here Here
                        Here Here Here Here
                          Here Here Here Here
                            Here Here Here Here Here
                              Here Here Here Here Here
                      Here Here Here Here Here Here
                        Here *Here Here Here Here Here*
                          Here Here Here Here Here Here *Here Here*
                            Here Here Here Here Here Here Here Here Here Her
                              Here Here Here Here Here *Here Here H*
                                Here Here Here Here Here Here H
                                  Here Here Here Here N
                                    Here He

                                                            Here Here H
                                                          Here Here Here Here Here He
                                                        Here Here Here Here Here Here
                                                      Here Here Here Here
                                                        Here Here Here
                                                          Here Here
                                                            Here

Here Here Here Here Here Here
ere Here Here Here Here Here Here Here Here Here
re Here Here Here Here Here Here Here Here Here Here
Here Here Here Here Here Here Here Here Here Here Here Here
e Here Here Here Here Here Here Here Here Here Here Here Here Here
Here Here Here Here Here Here Here Here Here Here Here Here Here Here
Here Here Here Here Here Here Here Here Here Here Here Here Here
Here Here Here Here Here Here Here Here Here Here Here Here
Here Here Here Here Here Here Here Here Here Here Here
Here Here Here Here Here Here Here Here Here Here Here
Here Here Here Here Here Here Here Here Here Here
Here Here Here Here Here Here Here Here Here Here
Here Here Here Here Here Here Here Here Here Here
Here Here Here Here Here Here Here Here Here Here Here
Here Here Here Here Here Here Here Here Here Here Here Here Here Here Here
Here Here Here Here Here Here Here Here Here Here Here Here Here Here
Here Here Here Here Here Here Here Here Here Here Here Here Here Here
Here Here Here Here Here Here Here Here Here Here Here Here Here Here
Here Here Here Here Here Here Here Here Here Here Here Here Here Here
Here Here Here Here Here Here Here Here Here Here Here Here Here Here
Here Here Here Here Here Here Here Here Here Here Here Here Here Here
Here Here Here Here Here Here Here Here Here Here Here Here Here Here
Here Here Here Here Here Here Here Here Here Here Here Here Here Here
Here Here Here Here Here Here Here Here Here Here Here Here Here Here
Here Here Here Here Here Here Here Here Here Here Here Here Here Here
Here Here Here Here Here Here Here Here Here Here Here Here Here Here
Here Here Here Here Here Here Here Here Here Here Here Here Here Here
Here Here Here Here Here Here Here Here Here Here Here Here Here Here
Here Here Here Here Here Here Here Here Here Here Here Here Here Here
Here Here Here Here Here Here Here Here Here Here Here Here Here Here

Here Here Here Here Here Here Here Here Here Here Here Here Here Here
Here Here Here Here Here Here Here Here Here Here Here
Here Here Here Here Here Here Here Here Here Here Here
Here Here Here Here Here Here Here Here Here Here
re Here

You are

Here.

So
know
the
kindness of the
universe. And know that there is great hope for us, if we
can find the hope inside
ourselves first.

Embrace the you inside you,
silence the voice that stops you from
being able to truly help yourself and others.

You can be someone who matters to others.

You can be someone who matters to you.

There is a kind of light that can shine in anyone, if they give
themselves the space to shine.

You need to remember because life has a way of making
you forget.

Now listen:

You are made of good things.

You are capable of incredible things.

You are a song the universe sings itself,
in every color it can imagine.

Some parts are sad.

Some parts are happy.

Every part of the song, is a part of you.

Listen.

Listen to the sound of the universe.

*Because the world needs
an infinite heart, like
yours.*

Or just a place where
everyone fits.

LISTEN:

Because we forget Time is
coming, even though he's
always coming.

We forget to listen to the
poem in the grass and the
light and the water.

We try to sound clever,
instead of listening to the
heartbeat in the stars.

And Here is what those who have
just arrived on Earth
cannot say:

"I'm sorry I made a mess,
I've never had hands before.
Don't get angry at me because I'm scared.

Hold me until it passes.

I heard a noise and I was worried that it was the end of the world.
You walked away and I was worried you were never coming back.
I was hungry and I was worried I would never eat again.
I was cold and I was worried I would never be warm again.
It was dark and I didn't know if the sun would come out again.
There were voices and I didn't know whose they were.
I've never done any of this before.

Love me, because I love you more than
anyone else has ever loved you."

There is a straight line that stretches back through every parent sitting in a chair looking at their child playing, knowing that their own parents must have looked at them the same way, and that one day the child you are looking at, will look at their own children like that, and you will be gone in all but the realization that you are joined by this imaginary line that stretches through generations.

"Wait, you're doing nothing wrong."

There is only one real sin in the end, and that is not being who you are, not listening to your soul, and forgetting who you wanted to be.

It's hard but without anything to overcome, we would not become ourselves.

Sometimes, this is all meant to be hard.

It is ok to struggle.

So do not ask for an easy life,

with nothing to do.

An easy life is not a good life.

And no one is always happy.

Here is one of my daily sadnesses:

There are men and women throughout
history who had far less than me,

yet I know

many of them must've been happier.

Here is something that makes me happy:

I believe that there is a restaurant somewhere in the universe that serves nothing but first meals and last meals.

The first time you ate with the person you loved.

The first time you discovered you enjoyed something, you always thought you'd hated, and the last time you ate with someone, without knowing it was the last time.

Somewhere, you can stretch every moment into a kind of forever.

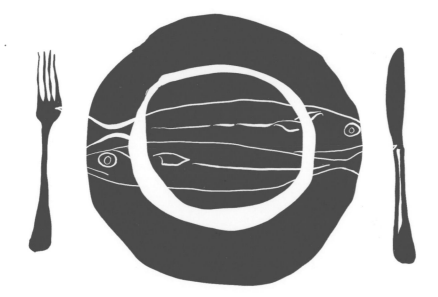

Here is the secret we all know:

We all want to love.

We're all afraid we are alone.

We're afraid no one will know who we were.

Because on some level, we all know you can die without love, without anyone, without even you knowing who you are.

(Unless you take care of you, and give yourself love.

Unless you meet yourself, inside yourself.

Unless you know yourself like you were meant to.

Forgive yourself for being you—
you have done nothing wrong and tomorrow is
another chance.

I swear, there is a day after, every day.)

Who could say,

"Show me the fix, the thing you did to make yourself whole, before you were broken.

Where is the God of everything that heals?

Can you pray to him?"

(What you feel is not brokeness, it is the desire to love yourself how you were meant to be loved.

It is your heart crying out.)

So pray to the God of everything that heals

—there is a temple in our hands when we hold
them together.

Because:

No one will ever tell you how great you can be.

You will never be asked to do something
incredible with your life.

You will never get a letter in the mail that says,

**"Dear you, please, do something important with
your time."**

Even if you do it quietly
you have to give yourself
the life you want.

In your head, in the dream, you are both the monster and the person the monster is chasing.

You are your fear and your love and you are the embodiment of all the things you feel.

Only you hold you back, or push you forward.*

*Sometimes, when we're awake, the monster is still there.

Maybe we can't see him as clearly, maybe he's not as obvious as he usually is, but he's there, somewhere, saying:

"You are not good enough.

You do not deserve to be loved the way you want to be loved.

Something will always be wrong with you, no matter how much you try and fix yourself.

You will always be looking for something you cannot find."

And our gut reaction when we hear the monster say these things, is to run.

But if we are the monster, and the person being chased, then we need to stop running because we cannot run away from ourselves.

You need to stop running, turn around and—hug—the monster. Because you are the monster. And the hero—the person running.

And everything between them.

You need to pull the monster close and whisper in its ear, no matter how scared you are, no matter how ugly the monster seems on the outside, no matter how much you think you can't, and say:

"You are good enough.

I'm sorry you're afraid.

You deserved to be loved the way you want to be loved.

There is nothing in you that needs to be fixed.

The thing you've been looking for, has been Here, with you, all along.

I am sorry I ran away from you. I am sorry you're afraid. I love you, honestly and sincerely, without end."

How?

Living is easy, you just look for the good in
the blades of grass
between your toes.

(Remember what I said: Listen for the poem.)

You just try and find something in everything, a myriad
of colors exploding outward from the center, and if you
open up your heart, it looks like unstirred paint in there,
it looks like someone loved you long ago and forgot to
stop loving you, even though you expected them to.

It looks like a way to be,
when there's no way left to be.

Because what else could you be,
but everything.

So go forward

        into bright light,

if you love hard enough,
your feet leave the ground
and you just kind of hang in the air
and that feels good, so love, because love is good,

        because it feels like you're floating.

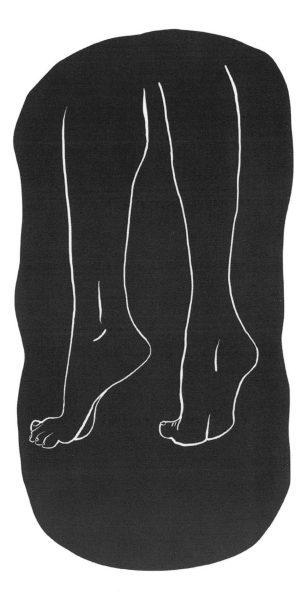

Maybe, in the story of your life, someone
has written:

You cannot say why you loved them.

Only that you did.

Only that you don't anymore.

But you cannot see the parts of you that shine when you're not looking, because all you see when you look at yourself is the picture other people have painted for you.

And that's not who you are.

You are the picture you paint, of you.

(You are still everything you could be.)

There, in the dream, you ask:

How?

How?

Break every vow that hurts you.

Take every opportunity.

Light all fires.

Turn all keys.

How?

They'll say,

"We can make miles if we hold our breaths and dive
beneath the sheets together, we can make it all the way
there and back if you trust me.

We can make it somewhere good.

Trust me when I say I love you like the light in
autumn loves the leaves, like a wave loves the sand, like
good loves bad, like everything we can still be
to each other."

How?

Pray for being aware that you're not waiting for anything and everything you are, you are.

Pray for being awake to every good thing.

Pray to the best parts of you.

How?

The world will always wear you down,
so let it wear you down until only
the good remains.

Hold on to the incredible parts of you
that survive.

How?

You love again.
Recycle your heart.
Someone out there needs it.

—Remember this.

Wait:

1. Have you told the people you love that you love them?

2. Have you gotten out of bed?

3. Have you drunk enough water?

4. Have you read something that wasn't on a screen?

5. Have you taken a moment to remember how important you are to you?

----------- *This is a checklist for being human.* ----------
----

Given enough time,
every building collapses,
every flower turns to ash,
every candle burns out,
every name must be forgotten.

This is not sad.

"Tell me about your silence."

It's a silence so big you could swim in it and blow up
bubbles from the bottom of it.

A silence so big it'd swallow you whole.

A silence so big, if you listen hard enough,
you can hear it roar.

"Let's talk about it another time."*

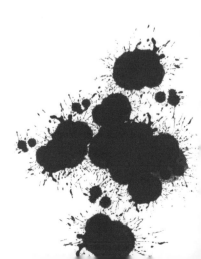

*If I'm honest, sometimes I feel like we've been trying to find each other in every life before this one, and this is as close as we've ever gotten. And I know now that we have to try again because we fucked this up. Maybe we won't even be born on the same continent next time, or the time after that, and we'll just spend those lives searching for something we can't find, miserable for reasons we will never understand. Until we get to try again. Until we somehow find each other in another life.

"What do I do?"

Be in the middle
Be in the middle of blue eyes,
Be in the middle of red fire, be the
peace

of every good thing.
of green grass, of clear rain.
good voice that asks for
and love.

I know:

Sometimes, you think you don't
deserve goodness.

But, I promise you,
we all have things
we think we don't deserve.

You deserve all the goodness you can get.

So:

Go find a pen
that only writes good things
about you,
go find the paper that hears it,
go find the person who loves you for who you are and
wouldn't change a single hair on your body, go find the
God of good deeds in the tips of a flower's petals,
go find the God of good conversation
at the edge of a tea mug,
go find yourself in the strange place
where all things live,
go find a way to be like dust in
light, suspended above the
carpet, go find a new way to be that doesn't make you
feel like you're trying to be
anything at all.

Take a moment, now, to be conscious of
what you're doing with your time.

If you intend to waste it, that's fine,
just be aware that you're wasting it.

Do not confuse being in the same room,
with spending good time with another
human being.

Do not confuse the distractions of the world,
with the world itself.

A silent bell is ringing.
Because every beautiful thing
is only Here when you are.

Please:

Do the hard work of being aware of the world around you, and what you think of it.

Take charge of your mind.

Silence your own critics but pay attention to harsh, good advice.

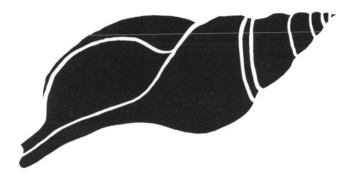

And listen to the kindest voice in your head.

Listen.

Here is what else I know about sadness.

There is a special kind of sadness that can only be found
in the confusion between who you think you are
and who you think other people want you to be. [§]

§ "Keep away from me."

"Just one more."

Why do we hurt ourselves more, when other people hurt us?
Why do we beat ourselves up, for feeling beat up?

Maybe the lesser pain you cause yourself distracts you from the bigger pain inside.

And it's easy to get stuck in a kind of loop of pain.

You're hurt, so you hurt yourself some more.

But the correct response to pain, is self-love.

When we're hurt, we need to take better care of ourselves. Not worse.

It can be hard to be conscious in the moment and remember to be kind to ourselves when someone hurts us. But you need to try.

Please.

Try.

You are the person who asks who they are.

You are a wonderer.

A searcher.

You are the person who asks who they are.

It's only the idea that everyone else KNOWS who they are that's causing you pain.

But no one knows who they really are.

You are an overflowing river that shifts its banks when the rains come.

That's why you cannot hold on to who you are.

And there is great joy in finding yourself
every single day and saying in your own voice:

"I know who I am. I am the one that looks for me.
And every single day, I find me again. I find myself
in the things I do and the things I notice. I find myself in
crowds and in solitude. I find myself in quiet moments
and at the top of tall mountains. I find myself in the
tips of waves, in forests, and in the books I read.

I find myself in leaves and rain and old photos.

Every single day, I find me again."

And if you find someone with a head made of colors and a heart made of secrets, try to love them like they need to be loved.

About being anything:

There are days when everyone needs you to be strong, even if you're dying inside, and you can only cry when no one's looking because you're petrified of letting them down.

And I know you know:

It can be so incredibly hard, just to be.

And hate?

Often, we hate people not because they have wronged us, but because they have reminded us of some secret part of ourselves that we don't like.

Maybe, making peace with the world starts with making peace with ourselves.

And sometimes anger is your body's way of telling you that you're ready to change things.

*And while your anger can be useful,
you have no duty to it.*

There is no register in the sky keeping track of whether or not you got angry as many times as you were supposed to.

You get to decide what eats you up.

And you have no obligation to kindness.

You can be kind as often as you want.

Kindness is not a currency, and if you treat it like one, then that is not kindness.

Within you, there is all the kindness you will ever need.

Not everyone wins the lottery,
but everyone who does
bought a ticket.

To live the life you want,
you have to be brave
and buy the ticket every single day.

Because there is a God of moments
and he passes quickly,
you have to be ready to pray to him,
even for little things.

And we must be gardeners
of all the things we find in our hearts.

And we are only alive in the moments where we either overcome or forget the everyday fear that we are not who we tell people we are.

And
And
And
And
And
And
And
And

Remember:

Living the life you want,
after you live the life you have,
doesn't actually work.

And now?

Show me how you tell someone that the thought of them spreads like a warm river through your soul, until it leaves through the eyes.

How do you tell someone that you would do everything for them.

How do you explain that there is no greater force in the universe than the love you have in your heart for them.

How do you tell them that you know now why you're Here.

Show me the words you would use, to try and say these things I cannot say.

And I will say them all.

This page is Here to tell you that it'll be ok.

This page is Here for every time you were told you cannot do it, to tell you that you can.

This page is Here for every time you weren't told anything at all.

So many people don't know:

People come with instruction booklets written on their eyelids and they try and tell you the things that make them work, and about what breaks them, about how to carry them, but the world doesn't listen, and we put people who shouldn't be in water in water, and we use the wrong batteries and we leave them on too long and we cry when we lose them, aloud,

"Oh if only we'd known,
if only we'd listened."

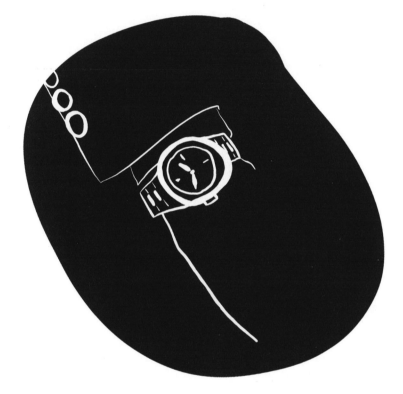

Don't worry, time must pass, even in the moments when it feels like it can't, or shouldn't.

"I wasn't thinking about anything."*

*I wonder at the stars every second I can't see them, knowing they're there and that the only reason we can't see them is that our own star blinds us. I wonder if people are like that. If there are just billions and billions of people out there who could shine light on us if we stopped staring at the thing that was blinding us. I wonder how people manage to love and hurt each other at the same time. I think about every person who passes me on the street and what it feels like to be them. I wonder if I'll ever do anything real with my life. I wonder if anything I do actually matters. I wonder how long it'll take for people to forget me completely when I'm gone. I think about the time it takes someone to answer the phone when I call them and if there's a conversation going on that I'm not a part of on the other end, where they're debating with someone else whether or not to pick up. I wonder how much of what people say, they actually mean. I think about how many ants I've killed in my life and I wonder if God ever thinks about us in the same distracted way. I wonder if anyone's listening when we pray. I like to think that I'd listen, if I could hear anything, at all.

We all intend to be perfect but
none of us are.

If only we could all see each other as we
intended to be, instead of as who we are.

And we're not everything we could be,
because we're afraid to allow ourselves to exist all at once,
because too many people have told us not to.

So try to carry on
picking the right strings on the guitar,
painting the right colors,
we don't know what they are,
we just know there are good songs
that haven't been written yet.
There is a child somewhere right now who
doesn't know that they will
shake the world
with everything they have to give.

There is someone trying
one more time,
and then giving up,
not knowing that they still had to
try one more time after that.

There is someone in all of us.

Here.

Here.

Here.

And you cannot hide your heart forever.

This is true of other people too.
Whether pure or impure, the heart shines through.

Give anyone long enough, and they will tell you
what is in their heart.

This is what the stranger you loved
did not
tell you:

"I know we are strangers but just for a
moment, I want to
pretend that we are in love, and that we
finish each other's
sentences and that there is no place we'd rather be than
right Here.

If it's not too much to ask:

Just for this moment, I don't want to be alone."

They wanted to say:

"You say I love you but we both know, when you say it, you are trying to remember the first time you said it, because every time you say it after that, is just a shadow of that time. And we know we change, we accept that, so I'm hoping that one day, we change into the kind of people who mean it again.

So I say, 'I love you' but I mean, 'I believe I will love you again, one day.'"

"I want you to discover a kind of paradise in my eyes, a way to swim into me and then feel us sinking together into some kind of newness."*

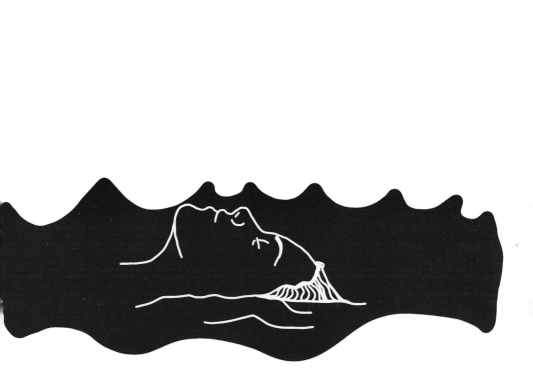

*Because I know you hate the way the world hurts sometimes and you're waiting for a time that it doesn't, because you can imagine the eyes of the person who might promise you that might happen one day and you don't fear them. And they are the only part of the world that you don't fear, they are all that you do not fear, you can't say love, because love is silly, how can you love someone you do not know, how can you love someone who doesn't e   x   i   s   t   .

But you can imagine being with them, driving in a car across a city at night, safe, warm, a song playing that you don't know, that you love for no reason   at   all.

In me
is a song
that no one
ence. In me is a song that no one
song that no one can
can silence. In me is
me is a song that
one can silence.
a song that no one can silence. In me is a song that no one can silence.
In me is a song that no one can silence. In me is a song that no one can silence.
silence. In me is a song that no one can silence. In me is a song that no one can silence. In me is a song that no one can
can silence. In me is a song that no one can silence. In me is a song that no one can silence. In me is a song that no one
can silence. In me is a song that no one can silence. In me is a song that no one can silence. In me is a song that no one
can silence. In me is a song that no one can silence. In me is a song that no one can silence. In me is a song that no one
ilence. In me is a song that no one can silence. In me is a song that no one can silence. In me is a song that no one can silence.
me is a song that no one can silence. In me is a song that no one can silence. In me is a song that no one can silence. In me
song that no one can silence. In me is a song that no one can silence. In me is a song that no one can silence. In me
ne can silence. In me is a song that no one can silence. In me is a song that no one can silence. In me is a song that no
e is a song that no one can silence. In me is a song that no one can silence. In me is a song that no one can silence.
e is a song that no one can silence. In me is a song that no one can silence. In me is a song that no one can silence. In me
is a song that no one can silence. In me is a song that no one can silence. In me is a song that no one can silence. In me
song that no one can silence. In me is a song that no one can silence. In me is a song that no one can silence. In me is a song that no one can silence. In me
lence. In me is a song that no one can silence. In me is a song
song that no one can silence. In me is a song that no one
can silence. In me is a song that no one can silence. In me is a song that no one can silence. In me is a
me is a song that no one can silence. In me is a
that no one can silence. In me is a song that
one can silence. In me is a song that no one
one can silence. In me is a song that no
song that no one can silence. In me is a
song that no one can silence. In me is
a song that no one can silence. In
me is a song that no one can
silence. In me is a
song that no
one

can
can silence. In me is a
silence. In me is a song that no one
a song that no one can silence. In me is a song that no one can silence. In
no one can silence. In me is a song that no one can silence. In me is a song that no
In me is a song that no one can silence. In me is a song that no one can silence. In me is

song that
one can silence.
In me is a song that no one can silence.
In me is a song that no one can silence. In me is a song that no one can silence. In me
silence. In me is a song that no one can silence. In me is a song that no one can si-
that no one can silence. In me is a song that no one can silence. In me is a
can silence. In me is a song that no one can silence. In me is a song
can silence. In me is a song that no one can silence. In
song that no one can silence. In me is a song
no one can silence. In me is a song that no
can silence. In me is a song that no
can silence. In   me is a

161

Back in the dream I ask you if you would burn with me,
if I burned, and you tell me that you've always burned for
me, and in the dream, I believe you.

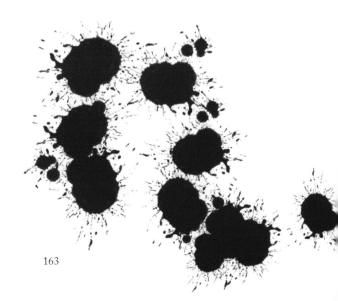

And I'm sorry if I hurt you by not being there.

I'm sorry if we let the clock turn while we weren't looking.

I'm sorry if you thought things were going to turn out differently.

I'm sorry because I thought things would turn out differently.

I'm sorry about getting old.

I'm sorry if you still miss me.

I'm sorry if I still miss you.

I'm sorry if there are days
I'd rather write about anything else but you.

Sometimes I'm sorry

everywhere

I go.

As a child, I would cry when someone took something
away from me.

When someone would say, "You have this. Now you no
longer have this."

You think I have grown up. I have not.

It still hurts when the things and people I love are taken
away from me.

The truth is, I have just learned
not to cry as much.

They will say:

"You can't fight this.

What are you doing?"

And you will reply:

"Fighting this."

They will ask:

"Why don't you talk?"

And you will answer:

"Because even if paper is cheap,

I've still spent a fortune on you."

They should've said:

"You should know: I kept every ticket.

Because I want to remember
every good place we went.

Even if the movie was horrible.

Even if the concert started late and it rained.

Even if the train took us
somewhere we were never meant to go.

I want to remember."

Surely, if love is a storm

then all you need to do

is be brave and get in a boat.

But you should know,

the best people

can't be found

on any map.

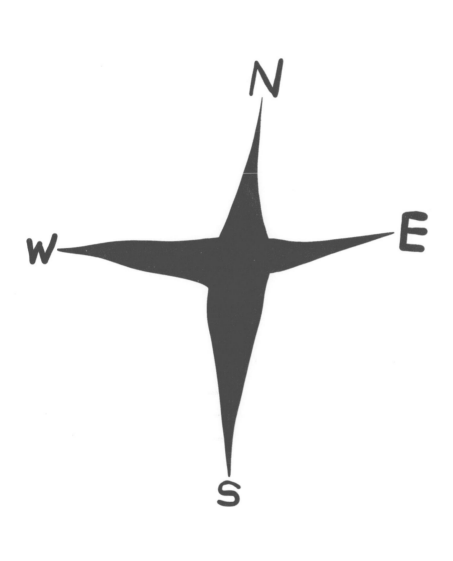

We could give each other's hearts participation trophies
and take each other home to our parents and say,

"Do you see? I told you I was real."

Because you make me real.

Remember:

You cannot nail words or water to a board.
All our words have ever done, is leave our lips, and
become air.

And I hope you get what you came Here for, even if you don't know what it is, even if you walk away feeling like you've left something behind.

I just hope you take something from all this.

How do you tell them?

"You have changed the way I love, by the way that you loved me.

I love differently now.

Maybe even less.

Maybe there's less of me to love.

Maybe there's more."

I want you to know
I saved up a little today.
Because I know I'll need it.
I was sad a moment today,
when I had no right to be,
when I should've been happy.
Because I need something for later.

I know a moment will come when I'm weak.

But I'll open the one
happy moment I saved today.

And live to see tomorrow.

—why do you talk to ghosts?

—because so often, the living don't listen.

Why do we talk to anyone?

Say:

"So when I die, bury me beneath the world, beneath landfills and flower beds, beneath my parents and my brother and my sister, bury me beneath my partner and my child, bury me beneath every good thing, so that if anything good happens, it happens to the good things and people I knew and know.

Because dying is for the living, and we all owe each other favors in the end."

"Do you know why this hurts?"

                  "Why does it matter if we know?
              Would knowing make it hurt less?"

"Maybe."

                "It hurts because we have hearts.
It hurts because we're human and we need to hurt this
              way, or we'd be something else."

And we're all looking for the one strange trick that'll make us happy. We're all hoping it's something we can buy or something that will change us just by thinking about it, like being in the now, or letting go
or enjoying what you have
or setting a goal
or taking up a hobby.
We all miss something or someone we're not supposed to miss. We're all pretending to be something that we secretly don't want to be. We all think we know what we want sometimes and we think we're dedicated and strong enough to get it, until we're distracted. We all stay up late at night writing sentences in lists that start with the words "we all" in the hope that whatever we feel, we don't feel it alone. Don't we?

Surely?

And back in the dream I play you
our favorite song.
I am looking straight into your eyes
and I say, "How are you Here?"
and you smile and shake your head
and become paper in my hands.

In the dream if I see you again,
I will shake you by the shoulders,
and be angry with you
and cry.

ches
of what swims i
the weight of what swims ir
the weight of what swims in my ches
weight of what swims in my chest. You do not
swims in my chest. You do not know the weight of what swims in m
know the weight of what swims in my chest. You do not know the weight
chest. You do not know the weight of what swims in my chest. You do not kno
what swims in my chest. You do not know the weight of what swims in my chest. Y
the weight of what swims in my chest. You do not know the weight of what swims in r
do not know the weight of what swims in my chest. You do not know the weight of what swims in my chest. You do not
the weight of what swims in my chest. You do not know the weight of what swims in my chest. You do not know the weight of
not know the weight of what swims in my chest. You do not know the weight of what swims in my chest. You do not know the weight of what s
swims in my chest. You do not know the weight of what swims in my chest. You do not know the weight of what swims in my chest. You do not know
know the weight of what swims in my chest. You do not know the weight of what swims in my chest. You do not know the weight of what swims in my ch
in my chest. You do not know the weight of what swims in my chest. You do not know the weight of what swims in my chest. You do not know the weight o
the weight of what swims in my chest. You do not know the weight of what swims in my chest. You do not know the weight of what swims in my chest. You
in my chest. You do not know the weight of what swims in my chest. You do not know the weight of what swims in my chest. You do not know the weight o
not know the weight of what swims in my chest. You do not know the weight of what swims in my chest. You do not know the weight of what swims in
the weight of what swims in my chest. You do not know the weight of what swims in my chest. You do not know the weight of what swims in n
the weight of what swims in my chest. You do not know the weight of what swims in my chest. You do not know the weight of what swims in cl
chest. You do not know the weight of what swims in my chest. You do not know the weight of what swims in my cl
not know the weight of what swims in my chest. You do not know the weight of what swims in my chest. Y
know the weight of what swims in my chest. You do not know the weight of what swims in my che
do not know the weight of what swims in my chest. You do not know the weight of wha
my chest. You do not know the weight of w
my chest. You do not know the weigl
my chest. You do not know the
in my chest. You do not kr
in my chest. You do n
in my chest. Yo
in my ch

194

You do not know
the weight of what swims in my chest. You
do not know the weight of what swims in my chest. You do not
know the weight of what swims in my chest. You do not know the weight of
what   swims in my chest. You do not know the weight of what swims in my chest. You do not know
the weight of what swims in my chest. You do not know the weight of what swims in my chest. You do not know the
weight of what swims in my chest. You do not know the weight of what swims in my chest. You do   not know the weight of
what swims in my chest. You do not know the weight of what swims   in my chest. You do   not know the weight
of what swims in my chest. You do not know the weight of what   swims in my chest.   You
do not know the weight of what swims in my chest. You do not know   the weight of   what
swims in my chest. You do not know the weight of what swims in my   chest. You
not know the weight of what swims in my chest. You do not know the   weight   of
ns in my chest. You do not know the weight of what swims in   my
know the weight of what swims in my chest. You do not know   the
my chest. You do not know the weight of what swims in my
ght of what swims in my chest. You do not know the weight
w the weight of what swims in my chest. You do not know
r the weight of what swims in my chest. You do not know
ht of what swims in my chest. You do not know the
wims in my chest. You do not know the weight of what
he weight of what swims in my chest. You do not
You do not know the weight of what swims in my
s in my chest. You do not know the weight of
of what swims in my chest. You do not know
he weight of what swims in my chest. You
wims in my chest. You do not know
u do not know the weight of what
f what swims in my chest. You do
ot know the weight of what
n my chest. You do not
eight of what swims
You do not know
what swims
You do

as
swims
what swims
eight of what swims
w the weight of what swims
not know the weight of what swims in
ou do not know the weight of what swims
my chest. You do not know the weight of
what swims in my chest. You do
not know the

"Sometimes, I hide in a coffee shop because I want to hear my name being called by a stranger, by someone I haven't disappointed yet.

And you can hide so much, you forget
what it's like to be found."

And you wanted to say:

"How can I help you, when what happened to you,
happened to you before I got Here.

You think if I went away, your problems would go away.

But I'm just a person. I'm not your problems.

Your problems, are your problems.

What happened to you, happened to you
before I got Here."

And you wanted to say:

"Every time I think of you, I try to think of a
blank canvas instead and I try to replace the
picture I have of you in my mind, and then the
hand of a ghost takes mine,
and paints a picture of you, anyway."

Maybe I will eventually unsay every good thing
I meant to say.

Maybe every good thing I meant will
become a blue line, stretching into infinity.

And I wanted to say:

"I have had

every conversation

we never got to have

with myself."

And in the end:

You don't have to know everything you know.
Forget the things that hurt.
No one's stopping you but you.

Maybe people will call you stupid when you
tell them you don't remember being hurt.

But sometimes, being called stupid would
hurt less than remembering.

So that your heart can open again.

So that you can leave behind every bad thing
that's hung on too long.

And in the end:

I hope you can close your heart like a
flower between these pages.

So that your heart can open again.

So that you can leave behind every bad thing
that's hung on too long.

And in the end:

I hope you can close your heart like a
flower between these pages.

In the end:

I really do hope you find what you're looking for, and I hope you find something new to look for after that, and I hope some part of you is always looking and that you discover that searching is something beautiful we all do.

I hope you never stop looking for *you*.

Every word you can say.

You hurt me.

You were meant to be kinder than you were.

You were meant to be better.

And I was owed more than this.

And you let me down, when I thought you were the only one who wouldn't.

But I will throw everything that hurts to the ground
and leave it where it lies.

But I will carry on, despite the world.

But I will become what I needed.

Because I am, and I will, and I can.

And so, I forgive you.

I forgive you.

I forgive you.

I forgive you.

I forgive you.

I forgive you.

I forgive you.

I forgive you.

I forgive you.

I forgive you.

I forgive you.

I forgive you.

I forgive you.

I forgive you.

I forgive you.

I forgive you.

I forgive you.

I forgive you.

I forget you.

Because I owe myself better.

And in the quietest moments of the world,
I can say that I love me.

I owe myself the best of me.

And no one can take that away.

Because everything I feel is real.

And I belong to the goodness, kindness,
and love that moves me.

I do the hard work of protecting my heart,
from the people who would hurt it.

And I'm awake to me even when I'm sleeping.

And lastly, you should know:

You cannot fix me because I am not broken.

And even though everything has changed, I am still more me than I've ever been.

When you close this book, your story will carry on,
in the kindness you show yourself and others.

When you close this book,
you will remember your heart,
and take it with you.

From Here, to there.

To there.

To there.

To there.

To good places.

To the truth that speaks in every moment.

To the little things that are real and matter.

To yourself, to the grass, to the poem, to the song the universe sings, to your great big silence, to your list of things, to your arms, to your mouth, to your heart, and at the end of everything:

Here.

Because in the end, *I am pointing at your heart, and you and every word you needed, were Here all along.*

Here.

Here.

Here.

Also by Iain S. Thomas:

I Wrote This for You

I Wrote This for You and Only You

I Wrote This for You: 2007–2017

I Wrote This for You: Just the Words

Intentional Dissonance

25 Love Poems for the NSA

I Am Incomplete Without You

How to Be Happy: Not a Self-Help Book. Seriously.

300 Things I Hope

*(If you have found one good word in here worth saying, take it,
and say it to the person who needs to hear it, today.)*